Learning Tree
1 2 3

Animals and Plants

By Hannah E. Glease
Illustrated by Bernard Robinson
and Richard Hull

CHERRYTREE BOOKS

Read this book and see if you can do the experiments and answer the questions. Ask an adult or an older friend to tell you if your answers are right or to help you if you find the questions difficult. Often there is more than one answer to a question.

A Cherrytree Book

Designed and produced by
A S Publishing

First published 1990
by Cherrytree Press Ltd
a subsidiary of
The Chivers Company Ltd
Windsor Bridge Road
Bath, Avon BA2 3AX

British Library Cataloguing in Publication Data
Glease, Hannah E.
Animals and plants.
1. Biology
I. Title II. Robinson, Bernard III. Hull, Richard
574

ISBN 0-7451-5091-8

Printed and bound in Italy by L.E.G.O. s.p.a., Vicenza

Everything is either living or not living.
Which things in this garden are living things?

All living things need food and water.

Food gives an animal energy to move around. It keeps it warm and helps it grow.

Plants need food and water to grow, too.
Their roots take in goodness and water from the ground.
Their leaves make food by using sunlight.

Put a stick of celery into a glass of coloured water and see how a plant drinks.

All living things need to breathe.
You breathe air in and out through your nose.
Your body uses a gas from the air called oxygen.
You breathe out a gas called carbon dioxide.

A dog breathes air too.
It pants for more air when it runs fast.

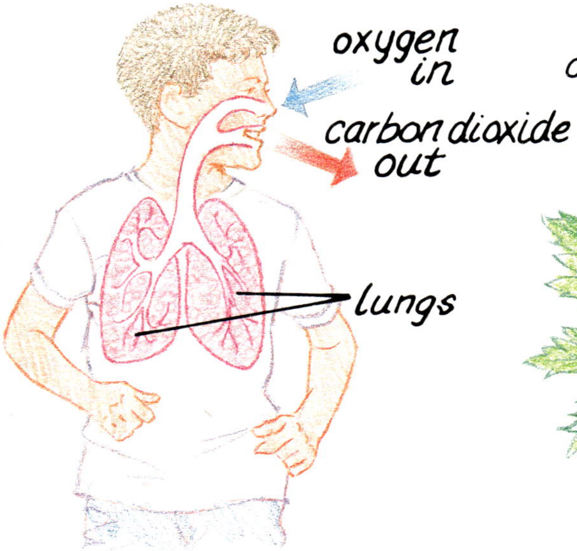

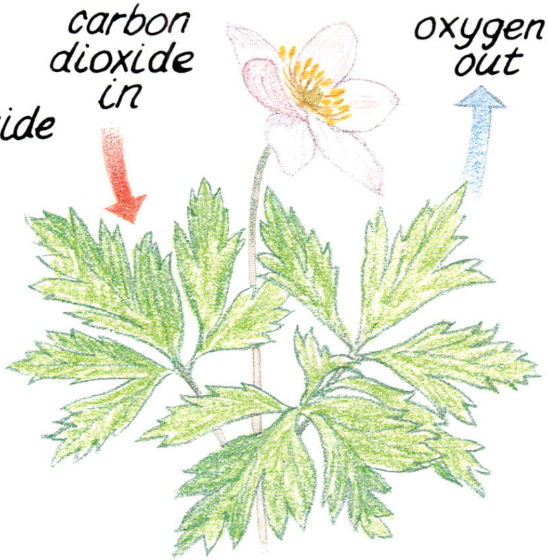

The air you breathe in goes to your lungs.

Plants breathe through their leaves.
They breathe in carbon dioxide.
They breathe out oxygen.

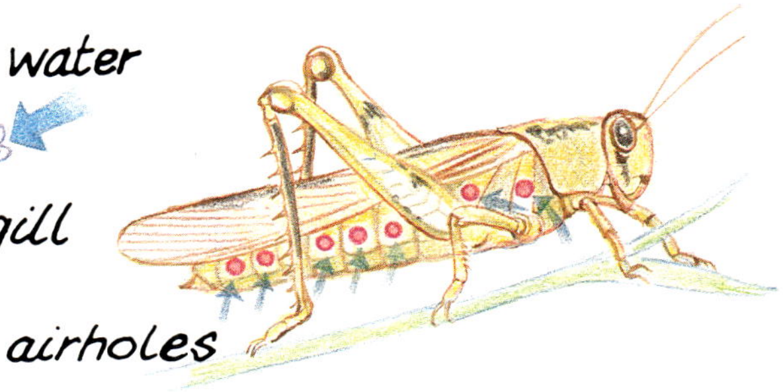

A fish takes in oxygen from the water with its gills.

Insects have airholes in their bodies.

All living things get rid of waste.
You get rid of waste when you go to the lavatory.
You get rid of waste gases and moisture when you breathe out and when you sweat.

Plants get rid of waste too.
Their leaves give off water and waste gases.
They store some waste in their leaves.
They get rid of it when the leaves fall.

Get an adult to help you fix a clear plastic bag over a plant.
Make sure it is tied tightly round the stem.
Watch what happens for a few days.
Where has the moisture come from?

All living things can make new living things.

Flowers have female egg cells and male cells called pollen.

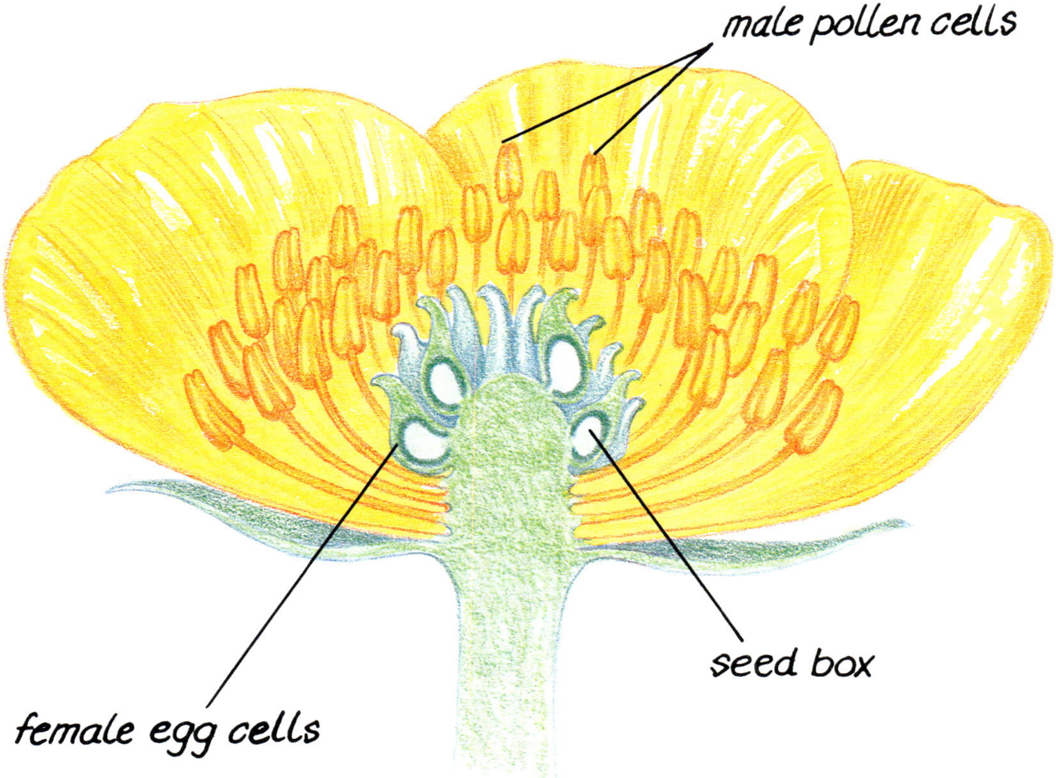

When pollen from one flower lands on an egg cell of another, a seed forms.
Bees often carry pollen from flower to flower.

A male and a female animal have to mate to make a new animal.
A male cell has to join with a female egg cell before a baby can grow from the egg.

Human and furry animal babies grow inside their mother's body at first.
Bird chicks hatch from eggs which their mother lays in a nest.

All living things grow.
Plants grow when a seed lands on the soil.
Plants go on growing all their lives until they die or are cut down.

Plant some seeds and watch them grow.
Put a measuring stick by a young plant.
Write down how tall it is each week.

Plant a bean seed in a jar with some damp kitchen paper.
Keep the paper damp and watch the bean sprout.
Does the root or shoot grow first?

Animals grow too.
But after some time they stop growing.
Are you still growing?

Measure your family.
Stick a long strip of paper to the wall.
Every three months mark the date and height of each person.
Who has grown? Who has not? Why?

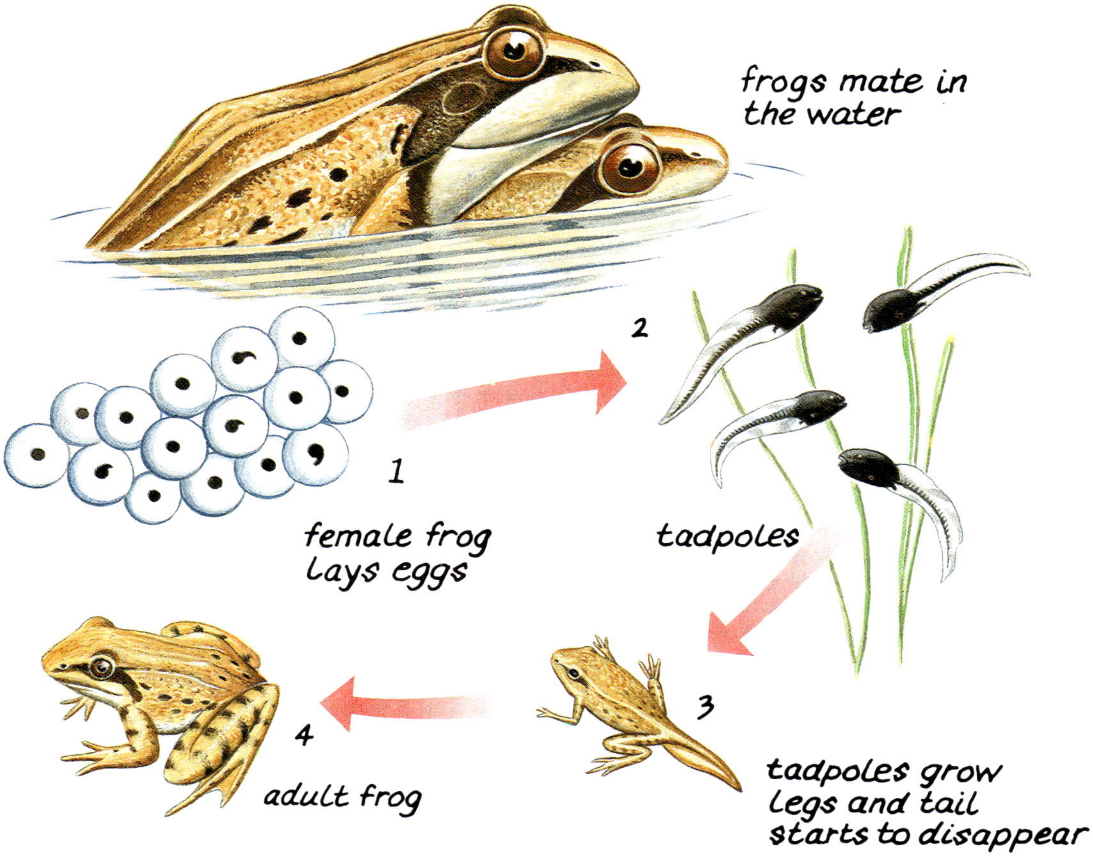

Some animals change as they grow.
The eggs of a frog hatch into tadpoles.
The tadpoles swim in the water.
Then they lose their tails and turn into frogs.

Butterfly eggs turn into caterpillars.
The caterpillars eat and eat and eat.
Then they rest and change into pupae.
Each pupa turns into a butterfly.

All living things move.
Plants cannot run around like you, but they do move.
They grow towards the light.

Put a sweet pea plant under a shoe box. Cut a hole in one end and watch what happens.

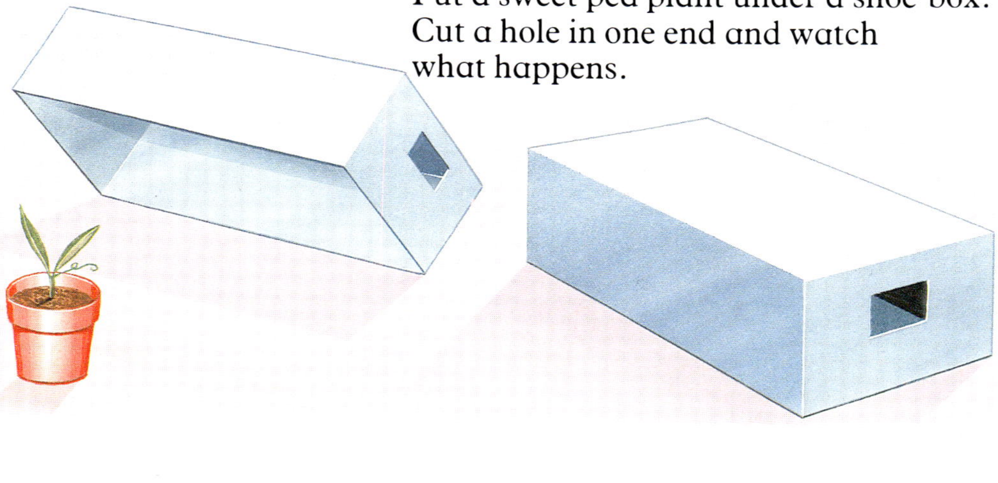

Plants and animals respond to life around them. A bird flies away if it sees a cat.

See what happens if you tickle a snail with a blade of grass.

In the end, all living things die.

More things to do

It is a good idea to keep a notebook. You can write down the results of your experiments and other things that you notice about animals and plants. You can also draw the plants and animals that you see. You can write the answers to questions in your notebook, too.

Questions
Write down any questions that you think of. The answers may not be in this book. But if you go to the library you may find the answers in a book there. You may find answers too by watching what happens.

Watch seeds growing
Put several layers of kitchen paper on to two plates and water them. Sprinkle some mustard and cress seeds on both of them. See how long it takes for them to sprout.

Keep one of the plates watered. Leave the other one alone. Which grows better? Which plateful will you be able to eat?

Grow a stem
A bulb is an underground stem. Roots and leaves grow from it. An onion is a bulb. Ask a grown-up to cut one in half for you from top to bottom and look at the leaves and roots. (It may make you cry!)

Put a whole onion in a jar of water. Put another whole onion upside-down in another jar of water and watch them grow. What will the difference be?

Collecting seeds
Plants flower and make seeds at different times of the year. Collect seeds from plants. Find out the name of the plant each seed came from.

Write the name in your notebook and draw a picture of it. Tape the seed to the book and write down the date when you found it.

Plant another of the same type of seed, if you can, and note when it comes up and when it flowers.

Plant diary
Find a young plant with a flower bud on it. Look at it each morning and each evening. Does it grow

more after rain? Does it change more on cold days or sunny days? Write notes about it.

Petwatching
See how your cat or dog responds to life around it. Make a chart like this:

ACTIVITY	RESPONSE
meal time	wags tail
door bell	pricks ears
thunderstorm	growls
warm fire	goes to sleep

Keeping creepy crawlies
You can find out a lot about small animals by watching them. Find a book that tells you how to look after ants or worms or other small animals. Make a home for them and keep notes about their behaviour.

Collecting tadpoles
If there is a pond near you, you may find frogspawn (eggs) in it in spring. Collect some in a jam jar. Transfer them to a bigger tank when you get home and watch the eggs turn into tadpoles and the tadpoles into frogs. You will need to find out how to feed them.

Butterfly or moth?
If you find some caterpillars, you may be able to watch them turn into butterflies or moths. Find out how to make a home for caterpillars. Then build the home, collect some of the plants they are on, and then collect the caterpillars. Do not take them off the leaves.

1

1 Have you seen any animals today? Can you remember their names?

2 Draw a bee on a flower.

3 What happens if a plant has no water?

4 What do baby birds hatch from?

5 What is a tadpole?

6 What do a butterfly's eggs turn into?

7 If you cut a fruit open you can see the seeds inside. What are the names of these fruits?

2

8 Draw a plant. Write the names of the parts on it: roots, stem, leaves, flower.

9 What happens if a plant has no light?

10 Look around the room. What living things can you see? What things in the room are not living?

11 Which of these is not a living thing: tulip parrot lion cactus doormat?

12 Imitate the way other animals move. Pretend to fly like a bird; swim like a fish; wriggle like a snake. See if your friends can guess what you are.

13 What do these animals grow into: kitten caterpillar puppy duckling foal calf?

14 Walk around a garden or park. Write down the names of six animals and six plants that you see.

3

16 Why do green plants need sunlight?

17 Why do animals need food?

18 Can stones make new stones?

19 Look at a leaf through a magnifying glass. Describe what you see.

20 Is a bulb a root, a leaf or a stem?

21 Name six animals whose names begin with the letter B.

22 What kind of an animal is a bee?

23 What kind of an animal is a penguin?

24 Human beings, monkeys, cats and other furry animals are mammals. Can you name some other mammals?

25 Find out what the word animate means. Look it up in the dictionary. What does inanimate mean?

26 Who eats what? Find out what each of these animals eats: blackbird slug earthworm elephant. Make a chart of your findings like this.

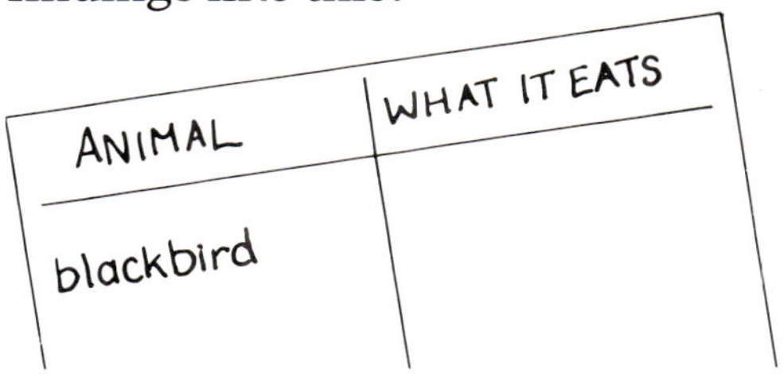

27 Find out what the word reproduction means. What two kinds of cell have to join for an animal to reproduce?

28 Can you name six things that all living things do?

29 What happens to all living things in the end?

Index